North American Animals

GRIZZLY BEARS

by Molly Kolpin

Consulting Editor: Gail Saunders-Smith, PhD

Consultant: Mark Haroldson, Supervisory Wildlife Biologist
USGS Northern Rocky Mountain Science Center
Interagency Grizzly Bear Study Team

CAPSTONE PRESS
a capstone imprint

Pebble Plus is published by Capstone Press,
1710 Roe Crest Drive, North Mankato, Minnesota 56003.
www.capstonepub.com

Library of Congress Cataloging-in-Publication Data
Kolpin, Molly.
  Grizzly bears / by Molly Kolpin.
     p. cm.—(Pebble plus. North American animals)
  Includes bibliographical references and index.
  Summary: "Simple text and full-color photographs provide a brief introduction
to grizzly bears"—Provided by publisher.
  ISBN 978-1-4296-8740-9 (library binding)
  ISBN 978-1-62065-314-2 (ebook PDF)
  1. Grizzly bear—Juvenile literature. I. Title.
QL737.C27K652 2013
599.784—dc23   2012000299

Editorial Credits
Megan Peterson, editor; Gene Bentdahl, designer; Svetlana Zhurkin, media researcher;
   Kathy McColley, production specialist

Photo Credits
Alamy: Robert Harding Picture Library, 15; Dreamstime: Al Parker, 11, Outdoorsman, 9; Getty Images: Photo
Researchers, 17; National Geographic Stock: Norbert Rosing, 13; Nature Picture Library: Eric Baccega, 21;
Shutterstock: Antoni Murcia, 5, Mighty Sequoia Studio, 19, Nagel Photography, 1, Protasov A&N, 7,
Scott E. Read, cover

Note to Parents and Teachers

The North American Animals series supports national science standards related to life
science. This book describes and illustrates grizzly bears. The images support early readers
in understanding the text. The repetition of words and phrases helps early readers learn new
words. This book also introduces early readers to subject-specific vocabulary words, which are
defined in the Glossary section. Early readers may need assistance to read some words and to
use the Table of Contents, Glossary, Read More, Internet Sites, and Index sections of the book.

Printed in the United States of America in North Mankato, Minnesota.
102011   006405CGS12

Table of Contents

Living in North America

Splash! A grizzly bear drops

its strong paw into a river.

It catches a salmon for lunch.

Grizzlies live near rivers

and streams in North America.

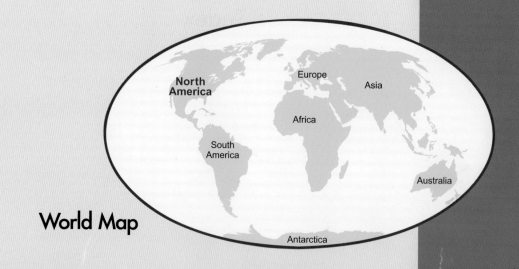

World Map

Grizzlies roam across

the northwestern United States

and western Canada. These

mammals live alone, except

for mothers raising their young.

North America Map

where grizzly bears live

Up Close!

Grizzlies are one of North America's largest animals. They can weigh over 800 pounds (363 kilograms). From nose to end, they grow up to 8 feet (2.4 meters) long.

Tan or brown fur covers
grizzlies' large bodies.

Grizzlies have a hump of muscle
between their shoulders.

This hump gives them strength.

Finding Food

Grizzlies use their sharp sense of smell to find food.

They smell rodents in burrows.

For larger meals, grizzlies hunt young elk or moose.

Grizzlies also eat berries, leaves, and roots. In fall they fatten up for winter. Grizzlies may eat for 20 hours a day. In winter they hibernate four to six months.

Growing Up

Grizzlies mate in late spring.

In winter females give birth to

between one and four cubs.

At birth cubs have little fur

and cannot see.

Young grizzlies stay
with their mothers
for two or three years.
In the wild, grizzly bears
can live 30 years.

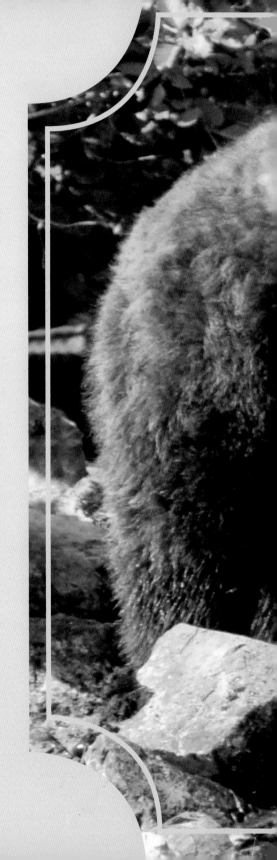

Staying Safe

The female grizzly keeps
her cubs safe. If people
or other bears are near,
she sends the cubs up a tree.
Then she charges the enemy.

Glossary

burrow—a tunnel or hole in the ground made or used by an animal

cub—a young grizzly bear

elk—a type of large deer similar to, but smaller than, a moose

hibernate—to spend winter in a deep sleep

hunt—to chase and kill animals for food

mammal—a warm-blooded animal that breathes air; mammals have hair or fur; female mammals feed milk to their young

mate—to join together to produce young

moose—a large, heavy animal of the deer family

muscle—a tissue in the body that is made of strong fibers; muscles can be tightened or relaxed to make the body move

roam—to wander

Read More

Owen, Ruth. *Grizzly Bears.* Dr. Bob's Amazing World of Animals. New York: Windmill Books, 2012.

Shea, Therese. *Grizzly Bears.* Animals That Live in the Tundra. New York: Gareth Stevens Pub., 2011.

Smith, Lucy Sackett. *Grizzly Bears: Fierce Hunters.* Mighty Mammals. New York: PowerKids Press, 2010.

Internet Sites

FactHound offers a safe, fun way to find Internet sites related to this book. All of the sites on FactHound have been researched by our staff.

Here's all you do:

Visit *www.facthound.com*

Type in this code: 9781429687409

Check out projects, games and lots more at
www.capstonekids.com

Index

Word Count: 222

Grade: 2

Early-Intervention Level: 17